KENDRICK LAMAR

TWO EXTRAORDINARY PEOPLE.

TRAVIS SCOTT

CONNECTED LIVES™

Ariana Grande | Camila Cabello

Ed Sheeran | Shawn Mendes

Halsey | Billie Eilish

John Legend | Michael Bublé

Kacey Musgraves | Maren Morris

Kane Brown | Sam Hunt

Kendrick Lamar | Travis Scott

Nicki Minaj | Cardi B

Photo credits: page 4: Kevin Winter / NARAS via Getty Images; page 5: Scott Legato / Live Nation via Getty Images; page 6: Chris McKay / BET via Getty Images; page 7: Robin Marchant / Tumblr via Getty Images; page 8: Andrew H. Walker via Getty Images; page 10: Mike Windle / Reebok via Getty Images; page 11: Mike Coppola via Getty Images; page 12: Kevin Winter / Coachella via Getty Images; page 16: Bryan Bedder / American Express via Getty Images; page 17: Kevin Winter / Coachella via Getty Images; page 18: Mike Coppola via Getty Images; page 19: Craig Barritt / Something in the Water via Getty Images; page 20: Santiago Bluguermann via Getty Images; page 21: Ethan Miller via Getty Images, Frederick M. Brown via Getty Images; page 22: Kevin Winter / Coachella via Getty Images; page 23: Kevin Winter / LiveNation via Getty Images; page 24: Gareth Cattermole via Getty Images; page 28: Paras Griffin via Getty Images; page 29: Randy Shropshire via Getty Images; page 30: Frazer Harrison / FYF via Getty Images; page 33: Kevin Winter via Getty Images, Matt Winkelmeyer / SXSW via Getty Images; page 34: Mike Coppola via Getty Images; page 35: Scott Legato / Live Nation via Getty Images; page 36: Christopher Polk / NARAS via Getty Images; page 37: Kevin Winter via Getty Images, Cindy Ord / Rolling Stone via Getty Images; page 38: Kevin Winter via Getty Images; page 40: Rich Fury / The Forum via Getty Images; page 41: Scott Legato / Live Nation via Getty Images; page 42: Ethan Miller via Getty Images; page 43: Kevin Winter / The Recording Academy via Getty Images; page 45: Scott Cunningham via Getty Images; page 46: Rick Kern / Samsung via Getty Images; page 47: hurricanehank via Shutterstock.com; page 48: Kevin Winter / NARAS via Getty Images; page 49: Christopher Polk / Coachella via Getty Images; page 52: Arnold Turner / Netlifx via Getty Images; page 53: Christopher Jue via Getty Images; page 54: Theo Wargo via Getty Images; page 55: Roger Kisby via Getty Images; page 56: Kevin Winter / Coachella via Getty Images; page 57: Bennett Raglin / BET via Getty Images; page 58: Bryan Bedder via Getty Images; page 60: Kevin Winter via Getty Images; page 61: Kevin Winter / Coachella via Getty Images; page 62: Kevin Winter via Getty Images; page 65: Kevin Winter / LiveNation via Getty Images, Bryan Bedder / American Express via Getty Images; background: Chris Wong / EyeEm via Getty Images; Kendrick Lamar head shot: Frazer Harrison via Getty Images; Travis Scott head shot: Matt Winkelmeyer via Getty Images

ISBN: 978-1-68021-793-3
eBook: 978-1-64598-079-7

Printed in Malaysia

27 26 25 24 23   2 3 4 5 6

TABLE OF CONTENTS

EARLY LIFE

WHO IS KENDRICK LAMAR?

Kendrick Lamar is a rapper, songwriter, and producer. His full name is Kendrick Lamar Duckworth. He was born in Compton, California, on June 17, 1987. Paula and Kenny Duckworth are his parents. Three years before Kendrick was born, his parents moved to Compton from Chicago, Illinois. The couple wanted to escape violence and gangs. Compton turned out to be violent too.

WHO IS TRAVIS SCOTT?

Travis Scott is also a rapper, songwriter, and producer. Jacques Berman Webster II is his real name. On April 30, 1991, Travis was born in Houston, Texas. He comes from a mostly middle-class background. His father has a master's degree. Both of his grandfathers have advanced degrees too. The artist's parents encouraged him to get an education.

THE DUCKWORTH FAMILY

Kendrick's family moved to California with very little. Their clothes were in garbage bags. They only had $500. An aunt lived in Compton, so that's where they ended up. At first, his parents slept in motels. There wasn't enough money to rent an apartment. Sometimes they stayed in their car. The couple had to save up for a place. Then they had Kendrick. For much of his childhood, Kendrick's mother was a hairdresser. His dad worked at KFC.

THE WEBSTER FAMILY

Travis's parents are Wanda Yvette and Jacques Berman Webster. The Websters got help from extended family too. When Travis was born, they lived with his maternal grandmother. She had a small house in the South Park neighborhood of Houston. Wanda worked retail. Jacques ran a business. In 2005, however, he became unemployed. Travis has an older brother named Marcus. He also has a younger brother and sister. They are twins. Their names are Josh and Jordan. Jordan loves that Travis is famous.

"WE WERE BROKE, BUT WE HAD US"

The Duckworths were on welfare and used food stamps. It brought the family closer. Even the time spent trying to make ends meet was valuable. Kendrick would go with his parents to pick up their food stamps. He told *GQ* that "if we didn't have that county building to walk to, I wouldn't have built that bond with my mother, or my father, to see that this is a family . . . we were broke, but we had us."

COMPTON MUSICIANS

Besides Kendrick Lamar, many famous hip-hop artists started in Compton. Dr. Dre, Ice Cube, and Eazy-E of N.W.A made a historic album. It was called *Straight Outta Compton*. The group has been inducted into the Rock and Roll Hall of Fame. Rappers Suge Knight, Tyga, and Coolio also got their start in Compton.

Ice Cube

FROM THE INNER CITY TO THE SUBURBS

South Park was a poor neighborhood. It was also violent. This shaped Travis's worldview. Both rappers understood from an early age how hard life can be. Travis is grateful for what he has. He doesn't feel proud of being from a tough neighborhood. When he was six, Travis moved to a middle-class suburb called Missouri City. There, he was surrounded by people from many different backgrounds. The rapper told *Complex*, "I adapted to . . . suburban culture, fresh culture, and diversity. I'm big on diversity."

Houston, Texas

9

A STRONG STUDENT

Kendrick was a good student. He usually made straight As in school. Teachers praised his excellent vocabulary. Still, he did not go on to college. "I could have went. I should have went," he told *Rolling Stone*. "It's always in the back of my mind. It's not too late."

PRIVATE SCHOOL INFLUENCE

Travis went to private elementary and middle schools. His private school classmates exposed him to new music. They showed him different viewpoints. At 17, he graduated from Elkins High School. It is one of the top public high schools in the country. After high school, Travis attended the University of Texas at San Antonio. He dropped out during his sophomore year.

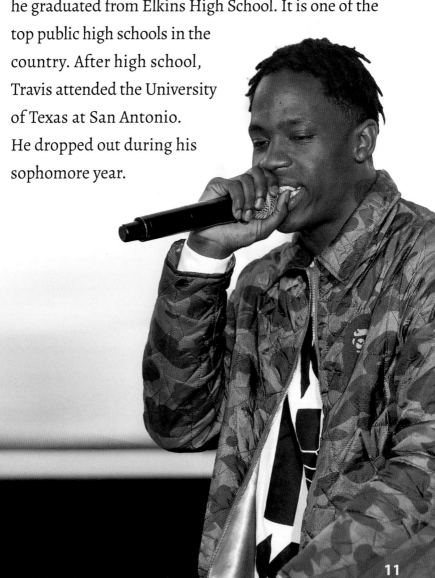

A MATURE LONER

Kendrick's first sibling was born when he was seven. In total, he has two brothers and one sister. Being an only child for seven years shaped him into an introverted boy. "I was always in the corner of the room watching," he said to *Rolling Stone*. The future star was also very mature. His parents called him Man-Man because he grew up so quickly.

A DRIVEN KID

Travis always knew he wanted to be something special. His mother supported him. By the age of ten, he was already friends with his future DJ. This was Chase B. The two met in high school. Often, they would go to football games together. The future rapper was already making music. He would even skip school to do it.

DEEP ROOTS

Both superstars are still tied to their hometowns. Travis Scott's *Astroworld* album, tour, and festival are based on a Houston amusement park he visited as a child. The festival was held across the street from the site of the closed park. Kendrick's songs are also deeply connected to his home. He wants his songs to show the reality of Compton. Showing that Compton residents are real people is important to him.

COMPTON BORN AND BRED

Kendrick had a mostly normal childhood. He played with friends. Activities like bike riding were common. Dancing at his parents' parties was too. But there are also vivid memories of the violence in Compton. As a boy, Kendrick saw young men shot and killed by gangs. Police were violent with him. The rapper also remembers the riots in South-Central Los Angeles in 1992. These made a huge impression on him as a child.

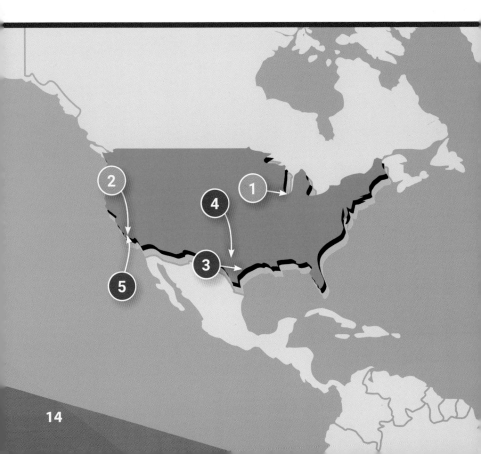

A HOUSTON RAPPER

"I feel like Houston is one of the leading things in music culture," Travis told *GQ*. He loves the traditional Houston rap sound. The city has had its own brand of rap music since the 1980s. Redefining Houston is also important to him. Travis believes that making a new kind of rap music will help. He wants people to see his hometown as a more important part of American music culture.

KENDRICK LAMAR

1. **Chicago, Illinois:** Kendrick's parents moved from the south side of Chicago three years before he was born.
2. **Compton, California:** Kendrick was born and raised in Compton.

TRAVIS SCOTT

3. **Houston, Texas:** Travis grew up in a suburb of Houston.
4. **San Antonio, Texas:** Travis attended the University of Texas at San Antonio until he was a sophomore.
5. **Los Angeles, California:** Travis moved to Los Angeles to pursue his music career.

CHAPTER 2

INTRO TO MUSIC

LISTENING TO HIP-HOP AS A NEWBORN

The Duckworths were not musicians. But Kendrick was steeped in hip-hop since he was a child. His father played rapper Big Daddy Kane in the car while driving newborn Kendrick home from the hospital. He also took Kendrick to the Compton Swap Meet. There, they bought cassettes and CDs. Prince and other singers were also played in the house. This helped the future rapper develop an ear for melody and using different voices.

MUSICIANS IN THE FAMILY

Travis's father was a drummer and soul musician. He bought his son a drum kit when he was three. Travis became intensely interested in the instrument. Later, he moved on to the piano. His musical past influences his hip-hop now. To him, melody is as important as rap. The artist is known for singing more than rappers usually do.

ALL ABOUT HIP-HOP

Dr. Dre and Tupac filmed a video at the Compton Swap Meet. Kendrick was eight years old. He remembers sitting on his father's shoulders watching the two stars perform. Tupac died soon after. Around this time, Kendrick began rapping. As a teenager, his musical hobby turned into a passion. The future star began to write about the Compton streets. "We used to wonder what he was doing with all that paper. I thought he was doing homework! I didn't know he was writing lyrics," his father said to *Rolling Stone*.

Dr. Dre

A FAMILY AFFAIR

It wasn't just Travis Scott's father who led him into music. His grandfather was a jazz musician and composer with a master's degree in music composition. His uncle plays bass. Another uncle, Lawalia Flood III, helped produce a platinum-selling record called *Fever for da Flavor* in the 1990s.

"I'M NOT HIP-HOP"

Travis says going to private school as a kid showed him other cultures. It exposed him to different types of music. "That showed me a whole other taste level of life. That's when I knew, [things are] way bigger than Houston, period. Which influenced me to just, like, tap into other things, stylistically," the star told *Complex*. He does not want his music to be tied to one genre. Travis told MTV, "I'm not hip-hop."

STUTTERING AND SHYNESS

Kendrick didn't always think he was going to be a hip-hop star. Until middle school, he had a stutter. He told *Rolling Stone*, "It came when I was excited or in trouble." His mother helped him get over it. She encouraged him to work on his shyness and fear of people.

A SOCIAL THEATER KID

Travis wasn't a shy young man. He was in a thespian society in middle and high school. Acting developed his confidence. During an appearance on *The Tonight Show Starring Jimmy Fallon*, Travis sang part of "Too Darn Hot." This song is from the musical *Kiss Me, Kate.* The star still talks about loving theater. Being in a Broadway play is a dream. Also, he wants to design a play around an album that he writes.

Jimmy Fallon

A NATURAL WRITER

Mr. Inge was Kendrick's seventh-grade teacher. The teacher often had the class write poems. It was Mr. Inge who showed Kendrick how talented he was with language. Kendrick began to enjoy writing. One day, Kendrick quickly finished a homework assignment. He still received an A. After that, he realized he had a gift.

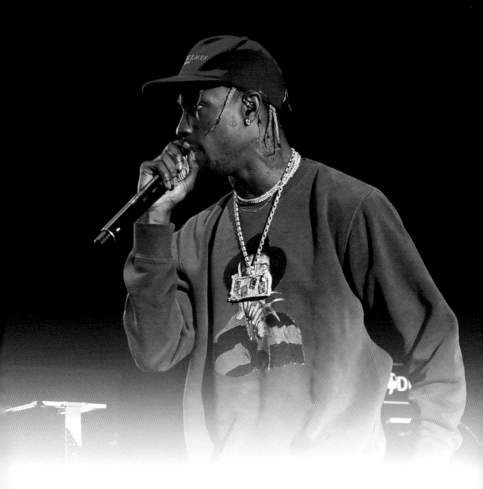

BECOMING A BEAT MAKER

Travis started making beats when he was 16. Beats are the music rappers perform to. They are made on a computer. The future star was unsatisfied with the beats that were available. He was also inspired by Kanye West's music. His mother bought him a new Apple computer. To make space for equipment, Travis got rid of his bed. Much of his music was made at home.

SAVED BY MUSIC

In some ways, music saved Kendrick. He told *i-D* that when young people see poverty and violence in the streets, "it just chips away at the confidence. It makes you feel belittled." Witnessing such violence can break people mentally. It started to break Kendrick. The artist spent a few years as an angry teen in Compton. Writing his difficulties on paper helped him turn his life around.

BIG AMBITIONS

While in high school, Travis wanted to express himself through rap. Rap lyrics could explain who he was. They told his story. He imitated what P. Diddy and Kanye West were doing. He was in a hip-hop group. But he mostly made beats at first. Travis wanted to rap more. So he studied it. "I was like, 'I got to get better,'" the star told *Complex*.

HOW ARE BEATS MADE?

The beat maker creates a full piece of music on a computer, usually with a keyboard hooked up. This person programs drums, keyboards, and other instruments and sounds. Existing music can be manipulated into a new beat too. This is called sampling. They sell the beat to a rapper or singer, who performs to it. A beat maker is different from a producer. Producers are much more involved in the entire songwriting and recording process, working with the artist who raps or sings over the beat.

FAMILY MENTORS

Kendrick credits his family for helping him
stay on a good path. "My mother encouraged
me to dream—she was very proud of my efforts," he
told *GQ*. His father pushed him to keep improving.
Other family members became mentors. People in his
neighborhood did too. They made sure he continued
in a positive direction.

A LITTLE HELP FROM HIS FRIENDS

Travis's parents really wanted him to get
an education. Once he dropped out of college, they
refused to give him money. After that, the star credits
his friends with his success. Friends would give him
money. They gave him a place to stay. "I feel like every
artist couldn't get somewhere without somebody, man,
like, if an artist told you he/she got there by himself,
[they're] just lying," the rapper told *XXL*.

PARALLEL LIVES

Wrote poems and stories

Influenced by the music of his hometown

Music has become about race and politics

Started making music as a kid

Has a superstar mentor
(Kendrick has Dr. Dre and Travis has Kanye West)

Worked at a young age with huge labels

Known for strong performance style

Was exposed to a rough
neighborhood

Played instruments

Influenced by a broad range of music

Music is more about personal life
and consumer culture

CHAPTER 3

RISE TO SUCCESS

DAVE FREE

Kendrick met Dave Free in high school. Years later, Free became the rapper's manager. He also became president of Kendrick's record label. Free told *Vanity Fair*, "The first time I ever heard him rap . . . I just couldn't believe it, since he was so young." The pair bonded over their love of hip-hop. Both also loved the TV show *Martin*. Free had a studio in his garage. There, the friends made music. They have been close ever since.

MIKE DEAN

Travis worked hard to get noticed in high school and college too. In high school he worked with Houston-based producer Mike Dean. Dean is known for working with Kanye West. He sent Travis's music to rap blogs. The producer also cold-emailed people in the industry. This means he introduced himself to them without having a connection first. Travis emailed one of Kanye West's engineers. His name was Anthony Kilhoffer. Kilhoffer eventually became Travis's manager.

K-DOT

Free helped Kendrick put out his first release in 2003. It was called *Y.H.N.I.C.* (*Hub City Threat: Minor of the Year*). Kendrick rapped as "K-Dot" at the time. He was 16 years old. A small, independent label in Carson, California, was the best shot they had. The label was called Top Dawg Entertainment (TDE). At the time, Free was working as a computer technician. TDE leader Anthony "Top Dawg" Tiffith called him to fix his computer. Kendrick's manager took the chance. He played the rapper's mixtape for Tiffith.

THE CLASSMATES AND THE GRADUATES

In 2008, Travis formed a rap duo called The Graduates. He paired up with his friend Chris Holloway. The duo released an EP on MySpace. Soon after, Travis formed another duo. They were called The Classmates. This time, he worked with a friend called OG Chess. That group put out several recordings. Travis produced for the duo. He promoted the music through his blog.

WHAT IS A MIXTAPE?

In hip-hop, a mixtape is a self-released album. Rappers release them for free. They are used for publicity. In the late 1970s and the 1980s, rappers recorded their parties and shows on tapes and sold them. Mixtapes outside of hip-hop are recordings of multiple songs for personal use. For hip-hop mixtapes, artists traditionally rap on top of other musicians' beats. Both are called mixtapes because they use other people's music. Even though modern mixtapes don't always use existing beats, the name remains.

TOP DAWG

Top Dawg loved Kendrick's mixtape. He said to *Vanity Fair,* "What impressed me was how advanced Kendrick was at 16 years old. He spoke from an adult perspective every time he touched the mic." TDE released Kendrick's next five recordings. Free encouraged him to begin using his real name instead of K-Dot for his fourth mixtape. The rapper's first record under his own name was an EP. It was called *Kendrick Lamar.*

STAGE NAMES

Both Kendrick and Travis rap under stage names. Kendrick used the name K-Dot for his first few EPs. He soon went back to using his first and middle name. His parents named him after Motown singer Eddie Kendricks of the Temptations. Travis created his stage name with inspiration from rapper Kid Cudi, whose first name is Scott. The nickname of his favorite uncle was also Scott. That uncle's real name was Travis.

DROPPING OUT

Travis dropped out of college without telling his family. He disliked school and thought about music constantly. After leaving school, Travis moved to New York City. The plan was to be a record producer. His friend Mike Waxx gave him a place to stay. Waxx ran the hip-hop website IllRoots. While in New York, he recorded music in producer Just Blaze's studio. His parents gave him money for books and supplies. Instead, he used it to pay for travel and necessities. After a few months, Travis moved to Los Angeles.

Just Blaze

Dr. Dre

DR. DRE

Around 2011, Eminem's manager Paul Rosenberg heard Kendrick's debut album. It was called *Section.80*. Free had sent it out for promotion. "Every word is so well placed, so thought out, so meaningful—there's no dead space," Rosenberg told *GQ*. Rosenberg brought Kendrick's music to Dr. Dre. The famous rapper also loved it, especially a song called "Ignorance Is Bliss." In 2012, Kendrick signed to Dr. Dre's label, Aftermath. Dr. Dre gave Kendrick valuable advice and tips. Kendrick learned about producing music and delivering lyrics more expressively.

"LIGHTS (LOVE SICK)" AND KANYE WEST

Soon after moving to New York, Travis realized his career wasn't progressing. Things started to change when he moved to Los Angeles. This was in 2011. He put out the song "Lights (Love Sick)" in early 2012. A music video for the song was released as well. It received attention. Epic Records soon signed him. Then Anthony Kilhoffer called. Kanye West had seen "Lights (Love Sick)" and wanted to meet Travis. West wanted the rapper to co-produce a compilation album on his label. Many artists would appear on the record. Travis would record a track for it as well. The album was called *Cruel Summer.* By November of 2012, Travis was hired as a producer for the label.

GOOD KID, M.A.A.D CITY

Kendrick's first major-label album was released in 2012. He was 25 years old. The record was called *good kid, m.A.A.d city*. It was a concept album. The music describes a day in the rapper's life as a teen in Compton. In its first week, the record sold 242,000 copies. *Good kid, m.A.A.d city* peaked at number two on the Billboard 200. Its release also earned Kendrick several Grammy nominations. These included Best New Artist and Best Rap Album.

T.I. AND GRAND HUSTLE

"Lights (Love Sick)" also caught rapper T.I.'s attention. T.I. used one of Travis's beats for his song "Animal." In 2013, Travis signed to T.I.'s Grand Hustle imprint. He kept producing that year too, working on Kanye's *Yeezus* and Jay-Z's *Magna Carta Holy Grail* albums. "Working on songs and going through the process of making a great album, being a part of that process . . . It helped me focus more," Travis told *GQ*.

T.I.

STRUGGLING TO ADAPT

Kendrick had a hard time adapting to success. He had trouble with self-esteem. So many of his friends were still stuck in Compton. As he said to *Rolling Stone*, "It brings confusion and insecurity. Questioning how did I get here, what am I doing?" When *good kid, m.A.A.d city* was released, Kendrick started keeping a diary. The rapper didn't want to forget his struggles when he finally made it.

STAYING FOCUSED

Travis wasn't successful right away. Keeping his mind on work helped him get there. He could have gotten discouraged or distracted. Instead, he kept working. Pressure and negativity did not get him down. "I'm proud of inspiring and not letting the ones I love down," Travis told *Clash*.

CAREER MILESTONES

1987
Kendrick is born in Compton, California.

1991
Travis is born in Houston, Texas.

1995
He begins playing music. His father starts to teach him how to play drums and piano.

2003
The rapper releases his first mixtape, *Y.H.N.I.C. (Hub City Threat: Minor of the Year)*. He signs a record deal with TDE that same year.

2012
Kendrick releases his major label debut and second full-length album, *good kid, m.A.A.d city.*

2012
Travis signs his first major record deal with Epic.

2015
He releases his debut album, *Rodeo.*

2018
His fourth studio album wins a Pulitzer Prize.

2018
Travis receives his first Grammy nomination for an album (he is nominated for three Grammys this year).

2019
He is nominated for eight Grammy awards and wins one. His first child is born.

2019
He performs at the Grammys for the first time.

CHAPTER 4

STARDOM

TO PIMP A BUTTERFLY

Kendrick released his second major album in 2015. *To Pimp a Butterfly* was its title. The record debuted at number one on the Billboard 200 list. It also broke Spotify's global first-day streaming record, with 9.6 million streams. On the album, Kendrick explores politics and race. Critics were impressed. *Spin* called it the "Great American Hip-Hop Album." *Rolling Stone* called it a "masterpiece."

OWL PHARAOH

Travis's first album, *Owl Pharaoh*, was a free mixtape. It was supposed to be released in 2012. Many issues delayed it. One of these was that Travis's songs used samples from other musicians. Permission from original owners was needed. *Owl Pharaoh* wasn't released until May 2013. Just before its release, Travis signed another record deal. This time he joined T.I.'s Grand Hustle. The record was nominated for a BET Hip Hop Award.

FINDING HIS VOICE

To Pimp a Butterfly is musically eclectic. Jazz, funk, and hip-hop beats were used. On the album, Kendrick spoke about slavery, racism, and Black culture. The songs mention important African American figures. These include Barack Obama, Nelson Mandela, and Martin Luther King Jr. That year, Kendrick received 11 Grammy nominations. He took home six Grammys. One was for Best Rap Album.

PRESIDENTIAL PRAISE

Former President Barack Obama listed Travis's "Butterfly Effect" as one of his favorite songs of 2017. Kendrick's "Humble" was also on that list. While president, Obama called Kendrick's "How Much a Dollar Cost" his favorite song of 2015. Obama also invited Kendrick to perform at the White House for the Fourth of July in 2016.

Barack Obama

DAYS BEFORE RODEO AND RODEO

Travis's next mixtape was *Days Before Rodeo*. The album was released in 2014. It had the hit singles "Don't Play" and "Mamacita." *Days Before Rodeo* was well-liked by critics. The album *Rodeo* was released the next year, debuting at number three on the Billboard 200. "Antidote" became Travis's first platinum single near the end of 2015. This song helped him hit it big. Now the rapper toured the U.S. to sold-out crowds.

THE PULITZER PRIZE

In 2017, Kendrick's fourth studio album came out. Like *To Pimp a Butterfly*, the album had strong cultural commentary about race in America. The record made history. It was the first hip-hop album to earn a Pulitzer Prize. Kendrick said to *Vanity Fair* that the prize was "not only great for myself, but it makes me feel good about hip-hop in general." Over a million copies of the album were sold. At the Grammys, it was nominated for Album of the Year. Kendrick won Best Rap Album. He also won four other Grammys.

GIVING BACK

In 2013, after the release of *good kid, m.A.A.d city*, Kendrick donated $50,000 to his high school's music department. It is now one of the top music programs in the U.S. As of 2017, 95 percent of students in the program earned college scholarships. Travis donated $100,000 to Workshop Houston in 2019. Workshop Houston helps educate young people in the city's Third Ward. His money is used to help students learn to make music.

BIRDS IN THE TRAP SING MCKNIGHT

Birds in the Trap Sing McKnight came out in 2016. It premiered on Travis and Chase B's Apple Music radio show. The album features André 3000, Kid Cudi, and Kendrick Lamar. This was Travis's first number-one album. The record went platinum. Its two singles, "Goosebumps" and "Pick Up the Phone," were hits too. Travis was recognized for his grand, complex sound. He later broke a world record by playing "Goosebumps" 14 times in a row live.

BLACK PANTHER

Kendrick made the soundtrack for the 2018 hit movie
Black Panther. Called *Black Panther: The Album*, the
soundtrack features his Oscar-nominated song with
SZA, "All the Stars." SZA is also signed to Top Dawg.
The Grammy-winning single "King's Dead" is also on
the album. Other songs feature South African artists
singing in Zulu. *Black Panther: The Album* was the first
Marvel soundtrack to have multiple original songs.

ASTROWORLD

During the summer of 2018, huge golden sculptures of Travis's head appeared at record stores and other locations across the country. These signaled the release of his third studio album. *Astroworld* was named after a Houston amusement park that closed in 2005. The album was his second to debut at number one. "Sicko Mode" also went to number one on the charts.

A RENOWNED ARTIST

Kendrick is one of the best-reviewed artists of the century so far. He has won 13 Grammys and has been nominated for 37. His breakout album *good kid, m.A.A.d city* has been on the Billboard 200 for over seven years, since 2012. Kendrick's work is even archived in the library at Harvard University. The rapper's writing has been compared to James Joyce and James Baldwin.

"THE VOICE OF A GENERATION"

Travis's music is very different from Kendrick's. Both are groundbreaking in their own ways. Travis is a talented musician. He is very skilled at writing hooks, or short bits of music that catch the listener's ear. Mixing musical styles is another one of his talents. For example, classical string instruments appear in his rap songs. Ellen DeGeneres called Travis "the voice of a generation" when she had him on her show in 2018.

A UNIQUE, THEATRICAL STYLE

Kendrick has become known for his unique performance style. The rapper is political, theatrical, and emotional. This style was highlighted at the 2016 Grammys. During his performance, the stage was set up like a prison. He and other performers wore chains. When it comes to rapping, Kendrick is known for being fast and furious. His ability to rap many syllables quickly has helped him stand out from other artists.

TOP BILLBOARD 200 ALBUM CHART

● KENDRICK LAMAR STUDIO ALBUMS

#113	🎵	Section.80	7/2011
#2	🎵	good kid, m.A.A.d. city	11/2012
#1	🎵	To Pimp a Butterfly	4/2015
#1	🎵	DAMN.	5/2017

AN ELECTRIFYING PERFORMER

The *Washington Post* has called Travis "one of the most electrifying performers of our time." He is fierce and passionate on stage. In one of his tours, Travis rode a huge mechanical eagle. His Astroworld tour had two stages. One stage featured a rideable Ferris wheel. Another had a roller coaster. "You have to be a whole experience," Travis said to *Clash Music*. "The fans are not around you all of the time, they only get this one moment, this hour to kick it with you. So I try to bring it to life."

● **TRAVIS SCOTT STUDIO ALBUMS**

#3	Rodeo	9/2015
#1	Birds in the Trap Sing McKnight	9/2016
#1	Astroworld	8/2018

CHAPTER 5

INFLUENCES AND COLLABORATIONS

WEST COAST HIP-HOP

Kendrick was first influenced by West Coast rap. His parents listened to Ice Cube and Dr. Dre. Tupac was another early influence. Kendrick told *Complex* that Snoop Dogg's "Who Am I (What's My Name)?" inspired him. "[The single] is probably one of the first rap records I really learned all the way." He later began listening to East Coast rappers. Some were Notorious B.I.G. and Jay-Z.

Snoop Dogg

INDIE ARTIST INFLUENCE

Travis has a wider range of musical influence than Kendrick. Musicians he loves include MIA, Thom Yorke, and folk act Bon Iver. Bon Iver was featured on his 2013 mixtape *Owl Pharaoh*. Missouri City was a diverse place. The rapper likes diverse musicians too. Some are genre-blending artists like Björk. Another is the trip-hop group Portishead. Movie directors Quentin Tarantino, Robert Rodriguez, and John Hughes are also inspirations.

Quentin Tarantino

SPECIAL ALBUMS

A few albums were especially important to Kendrick. DMX's 1998 album *It's Dark and Hell Is Hot* was the first album that inspired him to write raps. Eminem is another idol. "Eminem is probably one of the best wordsmiths ever . . . *The Marshall Mathers LP* changed my life." Eminem admires him too. He has referred to Kendrick in his lyrics.

Eminem

Kanye West

MENTOR KANYE WEST

Kanye West is "like my stepdad," Travis told
Billboard. They are personally and professionally
close. Travis helped produce West's *Yeezus* and *The Life of
Pablo* albums. West and Travis worked together as early
as 2012. The rapper helped Travis with *Owl Pharaoh* and
Rodeo. He raps in a few of Travis's songs too.

Dr. Dre

FRIEND AND MENTOR

Kendrick was a fan of Dr. Dre long before
the two met. They now have a personal
friendship. It was "more like [an] uncle-nephew kind of
vibe. Because . . . he shares the same story that I have,
a good kid in a mad city," he told *Complex*. Kendrick was
mentored by Dr. Dre as well. His label Aftermath has
been key to Kendrick's success.

Kid Cudi

KID CUDI

Rapper Kid Cudi is Travis's favorite artist. Travis said to *Rolling Stone*, "This dude saved my life. He . . . kept me on the right path. *That's* why I make music, *that's* why I go hard for the fans . . . 'cause this dude gave me the passion, the information, the insight on how to grow up and be who you want to be." Kid Cudi rapped on two songs for *Birds in the Trap Sing McKnight*.

Beyoncé

PERFORMING WITH BEYONCÉ

Kendrick performed with Beyoncé at
the 2016 BET Awards. This was a major
event. He joined her onstage for her song "Freedom."
Many thought the performance was electrifying. It
used African American imagery, music, and dance
traditions, including stepping. The performance began
with a recording of Martin Luther King Jr.'s "I Have a
Dream" speech. Then the two danced together through
a huge pool of water reflecting a wall of fire.

WORKING WITH DRAKE AND QUAVO

Travis has often worked with Drake. His 2018 single "Sicko Mode" features Drake. They previously worked together on two of Drake's songs, "Company" and "Portland." Rapper Quavo of the group Migos also made a successful album with Travis. It was called *Huncho Jack, Jack Huncho*.

BET AWARD PERFORMANCES

The BET Awards are known for performances that get people talking. Both rappers have been involved in notable performances there. In 2015, Travis jumped from a monster truck onstage while performing his song "Antidote." Then, in 2016, he produced his performance with Gucci Mane. It featured a black-and-white wintery stage. He tried to have actual snow on the stage but wasn't allowed. Kendrick performed "Alright" in 2015 using imagery of American flags and police cars. The performance generated a lot of buzz.

ATTRACTING BIG STARS

Many of the biggest names in music have worked with Kendrick. The rapper has made music with Jay-Z, Rihanna, Eminem, and Pharrell Williams. Beyoncé, Bono, and Maroon 5 have worked with him as well. He was featured on Drake's 2011 album *Take Care*. Kanye West invited the star on his Yeezus Tour in 2013. Kendrick also recorded a hit version of "Bad Blood" with Taylor Swift.

Maroon 5

The Weeknd

HITS WITH OTHER ARTISTS

Travis is also known for his collaborations. More than half of his Billboard hits are with other artists. The rapper has also been a featured artist on many platinum singles. He cowrote and performed on SZA's "Love Galore," released in 2017. Ed Sheeran recorded "Antisocial" with Travis in 2019. This was for the album *No. 6 Collaborations Project*. Many artists are also featured in Travis's own songs. T.I., André 3000, Young Thug, Justin Bieber, and The Weeknd have all collaborated on Travis's albums.

LITTLE HOMIES

Dave Free isn't just Kendrick's manager. The two also collaborate together on music videos. They call themselves the Little Homies and work under TDE. As the Little Homies, they have done groundbreaking work. Their video for Kendrick's song "Alright" was nominated for four MTV Video Music Awards. Kendrick puts the same passion into his visual art as he does in his writing and rapping.

Dave Free

FASHION DESIGN

Kendrick expresses his passion for visual art through videos. Travis uses fashion. He sees his whole life as art. "The whole aesthetic just has to be there. My clothes got to look like my music. My video got to be like my music," he told *XXL*. Travis has worked as a model and designer for fashion companies, including Alexander Wang, Helmut Lang, and Yves Saint Laurent.

HIP-HOP AND SNEAKERS

Sneakers have been important in hip-hop culture since the 1980s. LL Cool J made Nike's Air Force 1 shoes famous by wearing them on an album cover. Group Run DMC wrote a hit song called "My Adidas." They got one of the first sneaker endorsements. Kendrick also collaborated on a short film for Reebok. He says the brand "has a history of helping kids in the community realize their potential is limitless . . . and I wanted to be a part of it." Travis has collaborated with Nike on multiple sneakers, including Air Jordans and a Texas-themed Air Force 1.

SHARED COLLABORATIONS

In 2016, they made the song "Goosebumps" together. It was the second single from Travis's *Birds in the Trap Sing McKnight*. When talking about working with Kendrick, Travis called him the "best rapper in the globe." He also told *Billboard* that Kendrick said his music was "super dope and inspirational." "Goosebumps" went platinum five times.

In 2017, Travis opened for Kendrick on tour. From watching him, Travis told *Billboard*, "If anything, I learned how to take records and make them huge without changing yourself. . . . Just keep it pure."

Kendrick joined Travis onstage at Madison Square Garden for his Astroworld tour in 2018. The two performed "Goosebumps." This tour was one of the most lucrative of the year. It sold over 485,000 tickets in four months.

CONNECTED LIVES

Many hip-hop stars become successful outside of rap.
Childish Gambino is an actor and director. Jay-Z is a
producer and businessman. Kanye West has a fashion
line. This wide-ranging talent is part of what hip-hop
is about. Hip-hop is based on collaboration. It is varied
and diverse. Rappers draw from the wider culture and
use many different art forms. To its artists, hip-hop is a
way of life. Travis and Kendrick are on the forefront of
this masterful group of stars.

TAKE A LOOK INSIDE

NICKI MINAJ

TWO EXTRAORDINARY PEOPLE.

CARDI B

CHAPTER 1

EARLY LIFE

WHO IS NICKI MINAJ?

Rapper Nicki Minaj was born on December 8, 1982. Before she was known as Nicki, she was Onika Tanya Maraj. Her family lived in Saint James. This is a district of Port of Spain, the capital city of Trinidad and Tobago. The Caribbean country is made up of two main islands. They sit seven miles off the coast of South America.

WHO IS CARDI B?

Belcalis Marlenis Almanzar was born almost ten years after Nicki, on October 11, 1992. People know her as the rapper Cardi B. Her parents lived in the Bronx. This is a borough in New York City. It is north of Manhattan, where her grandmother lived. Cardi B spent a lot of time at her grandmother's home in the neighborhood of Washington Heights.

4

5

HOOD$TARS

Some members of Full Force created a new group in the early 2000s. It was called Hood$tars. Nicki was the only female rapper in the quartet. The other members were Lou$tar, Scaff Beezy, and 7even Up. Nicki didn't stay with the group for very long. Soon, she began posting more and more of her rap videos online.

LOVE AND HIP-HOP

While Nicki's career was taking a traditional path, Cardi B headed in a different direction. She became famous on social media first. The music career came later. Television producers noticed that many people followed her on social media. They invited her to be on a reality show. Cardi B was cast on season six of *Love & Hip Hop: New York (LHHNY)*. The show follows artists and producers. It also documents people who want to make it in the industry.

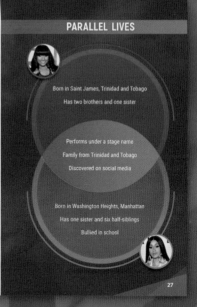

PARALLEL LIVES

Born in Saint James, Trinidad and Tobago

Has two brothers and one sister

Performs under a stage name

Family from Trinidad and Tobago

Discovered on social media

Born in Washington Heights, Manhattan

Has one sister and six half-siblings

Bullied in school

MORE ALBUMS

Nicki stayed very busy. The rapper from Queens kept releasing more albums and singles. "Starships" from *Pink Friday: Roman Reloaded* was another big hit. This album made it to the top of the charts in 2012. The next year, she had songs on the Hot 100 list 44 times. In 2014, *The Pinkprint* came out. Nicki's hit song "Anaconda" was on this album. "You should . . . always be trying to show that you're the best," Nicki said to *Billboard* magazine.

CONTINUED SUCCESS

Cardi B kept breaking records in 2019. *Invasion of Privacy* won a Grammy for Best Rap Album. It was the first time a solo female performer took home the award. The record also won Album of the Year at the BET Awards. The rapper from the Bronx had worked her way up to the top. "I feel like my life is a fairy tale and I'm a princess—rags to riches," she said about her success in *Harper's Bazaar*.

TOP BILLBOARD HOT 100 SINGLES

NICKI MINAJ

Rank		Song	Date
#3	🎵	Super Bass	4/2011
#5	🎵	Starships	2/2012
#2	🎵	Anaconda	8/2014
#10	🎵	Chun-Li	4/2018
#20	🎵	Megatron	6/2019

CARDI B

Rank		Song	Date
#1	🎵	Bodak Yellow	6/2017
#14	🎵	Bartier Cardi	12/2017
#1	🎵	I Like It	5/2018
#13	🎵	Money	10/2018

FOR MORE TITLES AND INFORMATION ⟶

CONNECTED LIVES™

ARIANA GRANDE
TWO EXTRAORDINARY PEOPLE.
CAMILA CABELLO
9781680217957

ED SHEERAN
TWO EXTRAORDINARY PEOPLE.
SHAWN MENDES
9781680217896

HALSEY
TWO EXTRAORDINARY PEOPLE.
BILLIE EILISH
9781680217919

JOHN LEGEND
TWO EXTRAORDINARY PEOPLE.
MICHAEL BUBLÉ
9781680217926

KACEY MUSGRAVES
TWO EXTRAORDINARY PEOPLE.
MAREN MORRIS
9781680217964

KANE BROWN
TWO EXTRAORDINARY PEOPLE.
SAM HUNT
9781680217902

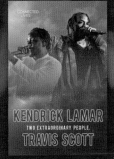

KENDRICK LAMAR
TWO EXTRAORDINARY PEOPLE.
TRAVIS SCOTT
9781680217933

NICKI MINAJ
TWO EXTRAORDINARY PEOPLE.
CARDI B
9781680217940

MORE TITLES COMING SOON
SDLBACK.COM/CONNECTED-LIVES